Distance Learning and Mature Students:
A Guide to Studying with The Open University

KATE SCOTT

ISBN-13: 978-1530626151
ISBN-10: 1530626153

CONTENTS

INTRODUCTION

Let me start by telling you what this book is not.

It is not a step-by-step guide to working your way around The Open University website or a book that goes into great detail about what courses they offer. All of that is available in very user-friendly terms on the website.

And besides, if you've already signed up for your Open University course, then I think you'll have plenty of reading to do without having to wade through another hefty tome.

This book is a practical guide to what you can expect when you sign up with The Open University; how to prepare yourself for studying with them; how to write essays; and how to do well in exams and get your qualification, from someone who has been there and done that.

I studied with The Open University for six

years to gain a Bachelor of Arts (Honours) degree in English Literature. I had been thinking about enrolling for a few years, but had been dithering, wondering if it was for me and whether I needed to put myself through all that work considering I was holding down a full-time job. But a colleague at work told me of his experiences of studying with The Open University, and I decided I would give it a go.

The main reason I dithered over enrolling was because I didn't really know what I would be getting into. Would I be able to return to study as a mature student and do reasonably well? Would I have the time to read all the textbooks or write all the necessary essays?

You're probably wondering the same thing. How much time will you need to devote to your studies and will you be able to manage? How much is it going to cost you and are there any ways you can save money?

But perhaps the most daunting part of mature student studying is realising how out of practice with learning you have become. For many people signing up with The Open University, it has been years, perhaps decades, since they wrote an essay or experienced an exam, and quite frankly, the thought of doing so again scares them. It is a little scary, but knowing this at the outset is the best preparation you can have.

Studying for a higher education qualification

shouldn't be easy, otherwise why would you bother? Studying can be a reward in itself; it can enrich your life, opening you up to areas of interest you might never have considered or even known about. It can introduce you to people who you would otherwise never have met. And it can make that dream job that much more possible.

You may even find that studying becomes addictive.

1 THE OPEN UNIVERSITY: IN BRIEF

The Open University was set up to provide a university level education to people who, for one reason or another, were unable or unwilling to attend a conventional university. Students can study with The Open University on a full or part-time basis.

The Open University was first established in 1969, founded by the Labour government of the day, and was the brainchild of Michael Young, who would later become Lord Young of Dartington. A planning committee was set up, made up of university vice-chancellors, education professionals and TV broadcasters, chaired by Sir Peter Venables.

Despite the new Conservative chancellor, Ian MacLeod's, comment that the notion of an open university was 'blithering nonsense', The Open

University was immediately successful and began enrolling students in 1971. 25,000 people applied in the first year. Just to put this figure into context, the total number of students in conventional bricks and mortar universities in the UK at this time was approximately 130,000.

The Open University's current student population is more than 250,000, making it the largest academic establishment in the UK, and one of the largest in Europe.

There have been several high profile and celebrity Open University students, including Lenny Henry (comedian), Joan Armatrading (singer/songwriter), Mylene Klass (TV presenter), Romola Garai (actress), Neil McIntosh (journalist), and John Reid (Labour politician, former Cabinet minister).

The Open University's headquarters are in Milton Keynes, and the majority of its tutors work at The Open University on a part-time basis.

The Student Body

The Open University is truly open, with entry available to anyone who wants to pursue a higher education qualification. There are not even set entry requirements for the majority of modules. All that is needed is for a student to demonstrate a willingness and ability to study at a higher education level.

Many students with The Open University are what is termed 'mature' - that is, a student above the usual university entry age of 18-25 years. Mature students are usually those in full or part-time employment, housewives or househusbands, retirees and senior citizens.

However, it should be noted that a recent trend is that more people in the 17-25 years age range are choosing to obtain a higher education qualification with The Open University. This can be attributed to two factors - the rising cost of conventional university education and the provision of teaching materials in digital, download-able formats, which are highly attractive to today's youth. This trend proves that The Open University is not a second-rate option for those wishing to pursue higher education, but a viable alternative to going away to university. Indeed, the Quality Assurance Agency for Higher Education has rated The Open University as 'excellent', whilst the English national survey of student satisfaction has put it in first place on two separate occasions.

The Open University is also open to people working or living abroad, prisoners, and armed services personnel, and is particularly proud of its commitment to providing higher education for people with disabilities or health limitations, who would be unable to study or cope with the physical demands of a conventional university.

Not every person who enrols as an OU student is doing so in order to obtain a degree or other higher education qualification. Some do it simply for the love of learning, to improve their minds, and develop personally. The Open University is ideal for this as students do not enrol on an entire course, but rather choose standalone modules, which when combined, achieve a defined qualification, such as a degree.

What Can You Study?

You can study a wide range of subjects, too many to list here, but they cover Arts and Humanities, Social Sciences, Business and Management, Computer Sciences, Psychology, Philosophy and Health and Social Care.

Go to **www.open.ac.uk/courses/atoz** to see the current prospectus.

Qualifications

You can achieve the following qualifications with The Open University:

- Certificate
- Diploma
- Bachelor Degree
- Foundation Degree
- PhD
- EdD
- MBA
- MPA
- MSc
- Med
- MRes
- PGCE
- Advanced Diploma

2 KNOW WHAT YOU'RE GETTING INTO

Studying takes discipline and if you cannot commit to reading the necessary textbooks, writing quality essays and submitting them on time, as well as attending an examination if the module requires it, then study with The Open University may not be for you.

Some modules have a great deal of reading to get through, as in the case of the *'Nineteenth Century Novel'* module for an English Literature degree. This calls on its students to read approximately 12-15 novels, preferably in the few months before the course starts! And these aren't short novels either; they're 5-800 pagers, with works by Dickens, Eliot and Collins.

If you read the reviews of each individual module, written by former students, you should be able to get an idea of how well you would cope with the workload, although every person's idea of what is acceptable is different. However, if you do begin to struggle with the workload, or real life just gets in the way, then it is possible to get extensions on essay deadlines and finishing dates for modules, should extraordinary circumstances interrupt your studies.

There is also plenty of helpful advice on The Open University website to help you plan your time and get through your course.

Bear the following in mind:

- You will be spending a lot of your time in private study

- You are solely responsible for managing your studying time

- You have to work out your own schedule for meeting deadlines

- You will have to actively seek out support if you need it

Your Studying Environment

Common advice will recommend that you have a

dedicated workspace for your studying. Whilst this is very good advice, few people have the luxury of an entire room in their home going spare and I believe it is best to study where you feel most comfortable, whether that means sitting on the sofa, at the dining table, or propped up in bed.

However, if you do want to do things properly and work at a desk, then here are guidelines for how your desk should be set up.

The chair

- Set at a height that allows elbows to be at a 90-degree angle to the body.

- Feet should be able to rest flat upon the floor. Alternatively, use a footrest.

- The chair should offer firm support, especially in the lower back or lumbar area. Chairs with arms make for more comfortable sitting.

The computer

- The screen should be set up at eye level or slightly lower, and at a 45-60cm distance from you.

- The mouse should be close to the keyboard so you do not have to stretch to use it.

Environment

- Well-ventilated

- Good natural daylight

- Directional desk lamp for night work

Finally, family may mean well, but it can damage your studying if you are being constantly interrupted. Try telling your spouse and children that when you have your Open University books in front of you, you are working and are not to be disturbed.

Motivation

As you have chosen to study with The Open University you are already probably well-motivated and determined to get as much out of your studies as possible.

However, returning to study can be a daunting business, and it is a very common experience for students to become dispirited by poor marks they get for coursework, leading to the feeling that they are stupid or lazy, or simply not up to the job. As your OU studying is pretty much carried out in isolation, this can be an easy trap to fall into.

While feelings like these cannot be prevented altogether, there are some steps you can take to try and keep incidences of these to a minimum.

Ensure you are interested in the module you are taking. Sounds obvious but you will find the course much more difficult to get through if you only took it to make up the numbers.

Make a note of your aims and objectives and what you will achieve at the end of your studies. Pin this up above your work area to serve as a constant reminder as to why you are putting yourself through all this work.

If you get stuck or find yourself struggling, ask for help, either from your tutor, other students, friends or family.

I would say that it is quite normal for motivation to slip as the module progresses. This is because the novelty has worn off and the workload significantly increases.

Who wouldn't get fed up by that?

3 TUTORS

You will be assigned your tutor shortly before your module begins.

They will be available to answer your questions, either face to face in tutorials, on the phone, or by email. However, be aware that most tutors also have other jobs, and you may have to wait a little while to get in touch with them or for them to get back to you.

I personally never encountered any problems with any of my six tutors, but I did read occasional forum posts from students who were unhappy with theirs, believing they marked them down on their essays, or penalised them unfairly, even that they were ill-equipped to be tutoring the module. If during your studies you are unhappy with your tutor, then you should to take it up with the appropriate OU authority.

If you attend a tutorial and do not 'take' to your tutor, it is possible to attend other groups' tutorials by arrangement.

Tutorials

All Open University modules offer tutorials to their students. Tutorials provide opportunities for students to meet face to face, and to become acquainted with their tutor.

These are entirely optional and attendance is not essential to successfully completing modules, but they are very good for students who find it difficult studying alone, and for those who enjoy meeting other people.

If you are in London, or any other major town or city, then tutorials should be fairly easy to get to. However, if you live somewhere that is a bit out of the way, you may have to travel a considerable distance for your tutorial, perhaps as much as 50 miles.

If you are not able to attend tutorials and worry that you are missing out on important and helpful information, don't panic. Often a tutor will email his or her students 'hand-outs', documents and notes of topics that were explained and discussed during the session.

As I said before, attendance at tutorials is not compulsory. I live in London and although my tutorials were not that far away, attending them still meant having to arrange to leave work early and cadging a lift off someone. I began my studies determined to make use of the tutorials, but as it turned out, I only attended two tutorials in the whole course of my 6-year studies. I still did better than average with my grades and got my qualification. From chats with other OU students, it is fairly standard for tutorials to be well-attended at the start of courses, and for this to fall off as the course progresses. The second, and last, time I attended a tutorial, I was literally the only person, other than the tutor, there.

It's okay to not be able to, or not want to, attend tutorials.

4 COURSEWORK

You may feel that you want to make the most of your Open University studying and get started straight away. You'll also probably have the best intentions of reading every bit of course material you've been supplied with from start to finish, whether you need it for your essays or not. I always started off with this intention, but it quickly faded as time ran away from me.

If you do want to make a start on your course reading before your materials are dispatched, then try to get hold of a copy of your module's course book/s from your local library. Don't buy the course books from Amazon or another bookshop though, as they are all included in the module fee and you'll end up with two copies.

Even if you do make a head start in this way, you'll be limited to how much work you can do, because you won't know which chapters of the books will relate to the essay questions. Most modules have between four and seven questions, and there are several chapters in course books that are not even touched on in the essay questions. These chapters may, however, come up in the exam (if there is one) so you may still need to read them.

Once you've chosen your module and paid its fee, there's little you can do but wait for your course books and materials to be dispatched to you. These are usually sent out about two weeks to a month before the commencement of the module. Once you get your course materials, you can start preparing properly.

If your materials contain audio CDs, I recommend mp3-ing these and uploading them to a mobile device, such as an iPod or similar. This way you can study whilst on your daily commute to and from work, cooking the dinner, or doing the housework.

To be honest, I never found the audio CDs and DVDs all that helpful in my studying. The truth is that The Open University can supply you with an almost overwhelming amount of information - the trick is sorting out just the bits you need.

Feel free to write in and mark up the course books. They are yours to do with as you please and these will be the primary reference source for your essays. The Open University acknowledges that while they encourage their students to look outside the supplied materials for their coursework, the textbooks contain all of the information that is needed for students to write essays and get good marks (unless the question you are working on specifically demands the use of outside texts).

However, it is worth doing your own research, at your local library, on the Internet, and at The Open University's online library, which you will be granted access to through your module website. The course materials are written by former and current tutors of The Open University, and they have their own opinions regarding the texts they examine. These may differ from your own and you may not want to be influenced by them exclusively.

Textbooks

On the module description, it will have been specified which books are included in the module fee, but depending on the module you are doing, there may be set texts that are not included but are still necessary for the course. These you will have to buy.

I studied for an English Literature degree and every module required the purchasing of additional texts that can prove quite costly. For example, with the *'Nineteenth Century Novel'* module, on top of the £750+ I had already paid, I had to fork out another £80 to buy the OU specified editions of the novels.

Here's my tip to try and keep costs down. Although The Open University will provide the ISBNs of the books you need and claim that you must have that particular edition, this is not always true. If you already own a copy of a book, but it isn't the same edition that The Open University specify, it will still probably be okay to use it. If you are at all unsure though, check with your tutor.

Another tip - if you hold off buying your books until mid-August, you may find that you can get hold of the ISBN-specific books second-hand. This is because the previous year's students have had their exam results through and having passed, begin selling of their textbooks.

Put the ISBNs of the books into Amazon's search field and then check out the New and Used books on the Marketplace, or keep an eye out on eBay for someone selling a batch of all the books. I doubt if you will be able to save many pounds this way, but even a few pennies may be worth it.

Coursework Reading

The difference between everyday reading and study reading is that you have to assimilate and digest the words you read for study purposes. You have to learn from what you read, use your reading to inform your arguments, and remember what you have read for when the exam comes along (if your module has one).

There are different aspects to study reading. These include:

- The amount of reading you will have to do - This will be considerably more than what you are used to, and may not be as enjoyable as reading the latest crime or romance novel.

- The difficulty level - Coursework will be written in an academic style, requiring far more of your attention than the average daily newspaper or paperback.

- The purpose - You're reading to gather data and ideas for your essays, not to be entertained. Be prepared to be exposed to different ways of thinking and new ideas.

- Reader engagement - You will be

expected to think about what you read, attempting to find the meaning in the writer's words, analyse it, and sometimes explain it.

In your reading, you may come across words that you don't understand. This doesn't mean that you are stupid - you're just reading a type of writing you are unfamiliar with, one that is formal and academic. If you find words you don't understand, simply look them up in the dictionary. That's what it's there for, after all.

You may have strong feelings about writing in books (many people consider it practically sinful), but these aren't novels, they are textbooks and they are supposed to be written in, marked up, and annotated. However, if you can't shake the feeling that writing in books is wrong, make notes with pencil that can be rubbed out, or mark pages with sticky Post-It notes. Be selective about your annotations, though, as you could get carried away and mark pretty much everything on the page, which will defeat the purpose. It is a good idea to have a pen and notebook with you while you read so you can make notes as you go.

This is very important - As a higher education student, you are not just expected to read and accept what you read, but question it too. When reading through your course books, especially material by critics, you should be asking yourself the following:

- When was it written?

- What argument is it making?

- What argument is it countering?

- Can you trust in the information being provided?

- Have key issues been ignored to support the writer's arguments?

- Is the work obviously biased?

- Has a strong argument been made?

And so on…

Remember to question everything.

Reading Critics

Many students, even experienced ones, struggle when it comes to reading and writing about the work of critics. Critics seem to occupy a rarefied atmosphere, writing in a highly complex style that is very often difficult to understand. Critics never use one word when ten will confuse you more.

Not only do they make your reading difficult, they can also outrage, disgust, or bore you with their opinions and arguments. It is important to remember to distance yourself from their arguments if you are to write about them objectively, especially if you disagree with them.

The best way to deal with questions that require reading by critics is first to establish for yourself the argument they are making. Summarise this in a few sentences, and highlight passages that support this reading. This should then make it easier to write about them.

5 THE MODULE WEBSITE

The module website is where you access parts of The Open University that are relevant to your current studies.

Your module website will be open to you only a few weeks before your module commences. It will display a calendar or schedule stating what you should be reading and working on at specific times, information regarding course materials dispatch, your tutor, and the student forum.

It also has a news section, which amongst other items, will advise students if there are any errors in their existing course material, and any relevant amendments.

The Student Forum

The forum is a chance for you to engage with other students who are currently studying the same module. How involved you want to get with other students is up to you. Personally, I found I didn't have the time nor the real need to make more than a few posts, but there were plenty of other students who were far more forum-friendly and giving of their time than I.

These forums can be helpful if you are a student who likes bouncing ideas off other people, want clarification on a TMA (what the OU calls their coursework questions) or advise on how to tackle a question without asking your tutor.

A word of warning, though - beware of assuming that other people are right and you are wrong! It is not unusual to be stuck on how to answer a TMA question, and to go to the student community for help. You might think you know what you should be doing, but just want some confirmation from another student in the same boat. But another student could point you in completely the wrong direction!

I remember several instances where my TMA question was peculiarly phrased and The Open University guidance a little unclear, and I wondered if I had taken the right approach in my essay. Reading other students' postings about the same question, it became clear that there were a number of approaches being taken. Who was to say which of us was right and which were wrong? In the end, I always went with what felt right to me, and this philosophy served me well, as I believe it will serve most people.

What I'm saying is trust your instincts, but if you're really stuck on a TMA question, check with your tutor rather than other students. That is, after all, what the tutor is there for.

That being said, the forum can be a handy tool for finding out about radio and TV programmes that may have some relevance to your course, as well as students sharing tips on note-taking, revision guides etc. Tutors also sometimes post on the forums and can provide clarification on essay questions if they feel that students are really going down the wrong path, although I believe there are limits to how much guidance they can provide in this manner.

TMAs

Coursework essays, known as TMAs, are due roughly once a month, with a slighter longer period given over Christmas if your course starts in October. While this may seem like an act of generosity on the part of the OU, the essay often due after Christmas is longer and more difficult than the others, so you still need to work like a demon on it.

A month may sound like plenty of time to read up and write an essay, but you'd be surprised by how quickly the time goes. This is especially true if you are working full or even part-time, as plenty of OU students are.

The way I coped was to allow myself no more than two days respite between submitting one TMA and starting work on the next one. Unless you're a really fast reader, a superlative note-taker and genius at creating submission-ready essays with a first draft, then I truly believe this is the best approach to take to avoid having to rush an essay in the last week and risking a low mark.

You will receive a TMA question booklet which will not only give you the questions and tell you how much weight they carry towards your overall grade, but guidance on how to approach them. If you follow this guidance, you can't really go off on the wrong track with your essays.

At the risk of sounding like a parent, always do your best on the TMAs, as they cannot be redone and they contribute greatly to your overall grade. If there isn't an exam at the end of your module, then they are, of course, all that matter.

Submission and Return

The Open University no longer accepts handwritten essays or essays sent through the post. It expects all its students to be at least competent with a computer, and all essays need to be typed, ideally in Microsoft Word .doc format, and submitted through the TMA electronic system. They will be marked and then returned in the same way. You will get an email telling you your marked essay is ready for collection on the module website. Login to your module, select the TMA section, and click the 'Collect' button to download it. There will be several documents there - your marked essay with comments by the tutor and a separate document giving more detailed feedback.

Your tutor will have marked your essay out of 100, made in-textual notes and provided you with feedback, telling you where you got it right and where you went wrong.

It can be an unnerving time when you receive your marked essay back, especially if you thought you had done well and get a lower mark than expected, but all you can do is attend to the feedback and apply it to your next essay.

If, however, you feel the tutor has been unduly harsh or unfair in his/her marking, then you can take this up with them. I never had reason to do this, nor know of anyone else who did, so I can't say if such appeals ever result in a changed mark, but the system of appeal nevertheless exists.

6 NOTES

You will need to become a proficient note taker when you study with The Open University to have material for your essays.

This is worth repeating - don't be afraid of writing in your course textbooks. They are yours to do with as you please.

Use a yellow highlighter to highlight important points or quotations, and annotate your thoughts and ideas in the margins. I used to star paragraphs that were relevant to the TMA question, and put 'VIP' alongside a passage if I thought it was worth using in my essay.

Don't attempt to write copious notes that are almost as wordy as the textbooks you're working from. Instead try to be concise in your note-taking, summarising the point being made. Leave plenty of white space around your notes.

This not only makes them easier to read, but means you can add to them later if other thoughts occur.

To speed up your reading and note-taking, use abbreviations and your own shorthand (just make sure you can understand them when you read them back later).

This is very important - When you are doing your reading and making your notes, make sure you take full bibliographic details, including the page number, of the source you are consulting. Make sure you do it at this stage, as you don't want to use a quote in your essay and then struggle to find where you got it from when it comes to the referencing.

7 WRITING ESSAYS

Essays are not easy things to write. Knowing what to include, how to structure an essay, how to word an essay - all of these take practice, and those returning to education after a long hiatus may find it difficult to know how to start.

The essay writing process involves the follow stages:

- Reading and understanding the TMA question

- Reading the essay guidance

- Reviewing the relevant chapters in the course books

- Establishing your argument and gathering evidence

- Creating an essay plan

- Writing your first draft

- Polishing your first draft

- Reviewing your second draft

- Submitting your final draft

An essay should include an introduction, your arguments or evidence, a conclusion and a bibliography. To make sure you get the structure right, create an essay plan before you start.

Make sure you understand the question. Sometimes these can seem incomprehensible, as if the writer has gone out of his way to make it difficult for you. Try to isolate the important words in the question.

Some examples of important words in essay questions:

- Analyse - Methodically examine the subject of the question, explain and interpret.

- Compare - Describe similarities and differences between two or more subjects, sometimes demonstrating a preference for one or the other.

- Contrast - Describe the differences between two or more subjects.

- Discuss - Consider a subject, then define and explain whichever argument you take in support or rejection.

- Examine - Describe a subject in detail, but not necessarily make a judgement or argument.

- Explore - Similar to 'examine', but requires a wider range of points.

- Evaluate - Make a judgement about a (critic's) opinion or subject.

Be selective in your points. Most essays are approximately 1,500 to 4,000 words long, depending on the course level, and you will frequently wonder how you can possibly fit in all you have to say. It is far better to make detailed arguments on a few points than make vague arguments on several.

Here's a tip for editing your first draft. Have

the essay Word document open and open up a blank document alongside. This is easier if you have more than one monitor, but if you have only the one, just reduce the size of each window to fit them both on.

If your first draft is more than the required word count (and it probably will be), you can cut superfluous passages and paste them into the blank document. This way they can be retrieved should you decide you want them back in your essay. Save this cut and pasted document under the name 'Discards'.

If your essays continually seem to be falling short of the required word count, it sounds like you're not making enough notes. I suggest a brainstorming session. Brainstorming is a good way to find ideas for starting your essay. Get yourself a sheet of paper, the bigger the better, and write the key word or phrase from the TMA question in the middle of the page, and then just keep writing down anything and everything that comes to mind. This will throw up lots of ideas, some of them useful, some not, but you will at least have something to work from, which is far better than simply staring at a blank page.

Don't be afraid of putting your own opinion into your essays, especially in Level 3 courses. As long as you can back up your opinion, then it should be welcomed by your tutor as it shows you are really learning from your studies to the point where you feel confident to make your own arguments. You may even come across some essays that specifically ask for your opinion, such as '*Do you agree with this statement?*'

Essays need to be written in a formal language, not quite legalese, but definitely not in the mould of blog posts or texts. Contractions such as 'don't' 'it's', and so on are not acceptable and should be written in full.

When you have what you consider to be a final draft, leave it for a day or two. Then look it over, checking for errors and making sure your arguments are clear and well supported. If you know that your spelling, punctuation and grammar are weak, get a relative, friend, or even a professional proofreader to check your essay over for you before submitting it.

You'll probably get to the stage when you are just fed up with the damn thing, and want to get rid of it. If you do reach this stage, it's unlikely that any more work will make that much difference (everything can be improved, but deadlines mean you can't be a perfectionist). If you've had enough of a TMA and you're reasonably satisfied with it, send it off, leave it a few days, and then start work on the next one.

Tips

- To make sure you know how the electronic TMA system works, it can be helpful to submit a dummy essay to test it.

- Don't try to work for hours at your essay - it will be counter-productive. Take regular breaks, get up and make a cup of tea for fifteen minutes, take the dog for a walk etc.

- Don't attempt to write a perfect essay first time, just focus on getting your argument down. Your essay will need to go through a minimum of two drafts before it is suitable for submission.

- You will need to decide whether your first draft is best attempted on paper or on screen. Maybe a combination of both.

- I advise getting someone else to read your finished essay before submission, asking them to let you know whether they found it easy to read, clearly argued, and a natural, succinct conclusion reached and articulated.

Main points to remember

- Your essay must be well-presented, correctly formatted, with perfect spelling and punctuation.

- Your essay should be based on your coursework reading to prove that you have covered and understood what you have read.

- You should write in a formal way, but do not use long words or complicated language designed to impress if you can make your point with more clarity by using simpler language.

- Always try to meet your deadline (only forgivable in extreme circumstances).

- Structure it properly – introduction / argument / conclusion.

- Answer the question – don't digress.

- Make sure all your evidence / quoted material is relevant.

- You must avoid plagiarism - otherwise known, in essay terms, as cheating. If you are using someone else's words in your essay, these should be put in single quotation marks (') and referenced. If you copy verbatim without doing this, you will be penalised, or your work disqualified.

■ Leave yourself enough time to present a final draft rather than a first draft.

For a more in-depth guide to tackling essays, please see my companion book, '*How to Write Essays: A Guide for Mature Students Who Have Forgotten How*'.

Referencing

Of great importance is the referencing of quotations used in your essays. I have to say I found this one of the most irksome tasks, but failure to do this accurately will result in you being penalised. The Open University follows the Harvard system of referencing. This is an author and date system, referencing the materials that have been cited in the essay.

For example:

Ryan, K. (2000). *Shakespeare: Texts and*

Contexts. Milton Keynes: The Open University.

Bibliographic details for books/eBooks should include:

- Author's surname and initials
- Publication date
- Book title
- Publishers name
- Place of publication
- Page numbers of specific info or quotations, if applicable

Bibliographic details for journals/magazines should include:

- Author's surname and initials
- Article title
- Journal/magazine title
- Journal/magazine volume and/or number
- Journal/magazine's article page numbers

Bibliographic details for information retrieved from a website:

- Author's surname and initials (if available)
- Publication date (or last revised date)
- Document title

- Title of complete work (if applicable)
- URL (website address)
- Date site was accessed

There may not be the need to put full references in against every quote. An essay will be full of quotes, many of them from the same book. If you have a paragraph that contains several quotes from the same book, instead of putting the full reference each time, you should simply put (ibid.) and if it is a quote from the same book but on a different page, (ibid. p.34) for example. Ibid means the same as what came before.

This is only the case within paragraphs. Every time a new paragraph is opened, any quotes contained within it must be considered as standalones, and full referencing given, at least in the first instance.

If you have read other books in research for your essay, but not quoted from them or referred to them in your text, you can still include them in your bibliography, but it is not necessary, perhaps not even advisable, as some tutors may have particular feelings about this. I seem to remember I once unwittingly included a book in my bibliography that I hadn't referred to in my essay, and this was pointed out by my tutor. I'm not saying I lost marks for it, but the only effect it had was negative. Long bibliographies do not create the impression that you've really done your homework so don't think of making them long for effect.

Referencing can be the most frustrating and tiresome aspect of essay writing. It is also however, one of the most necessary, but I didn't insert perfect references until my final draft. The way I worked was to write the essay and when I used a quote I simply put the page number and abbreviations of the title in brackets so I knew where it had come from. Then at the end, when the essay was written, I would go through and add in the proper referencing. I found this easier than trying to reference correctly as I went along, and bearing in mind that you will be, or should be, redrafting the essay, it can make it easier to keep quotes and their relevant references together.

Sample Essay

Taken from A210 Approaching Literature

This course has now been discontinued, which is why I feel able to include this TMA question and essay here, in their entirety. This example includes a suggested format for submission.

~

[Your name] [Personal identifier number]

TMA 07

Women offer an alternative set of values to those which prevail in the male world. Discuss with reference to Othello and The Rover, bearing in mind the different genres of those plays.

Despite different genres, both Othello and The Rover, explore similar themes of love, jealousy, deception, duty and honour. Whilst loss of honour has fatal consequences in Othello, the principle and perception of honour is constantly being challenged in The Rover by both men and women.

Othello is a tragedy, the definition of which

is the downfall of a noble person. Inherent in that nobility is the concept of honour. It is Cassio who demonstrates the worth of honour in a man's person. The loss of his lieutenancy degrades him, so that he feels he has suffered a bodily hurt 'past all surgery.' (Shakespeare, W., (2005) p. 51, l.253). He describes what reputation, and by extension, honour, means to him and speaks for all men of his caste with 'I have lost the immortal part of myself, and what remains is bestial,' (ibid, ll.256-7). Ironically, it is in part the attempt to restore his honour that contributes to the death of Desdemona for her supposed loss of honour.

In this patriarchal society, it is Brabantio's right to expect obedience and duty in his daughter, as he demands of Desdemona, by asking 'Do you perceive in all this company/Where most you owe obedience?' (Shakespeare, W., (2005) p. 22 ll.179-180). Desdemona challenges this, not denying that she does owe obedience, but arguing that she has transferred it from her father to her husband, 'as my mother showed/To you, preferring you before her father,' (ibid. p.23, ll. 184-5). That Desdemona should take for a husband 'what she feared to look on!' (ibid. p.20, l.98) seems not so galling to Brabantio as that the marriage should 't'incur a general mock,' (ibid. p.15, l.69) and thus disgrace him in the eyes of his peers. It is in fact, Brabantio's parting words that sows the seed for Othello's later belief in his wife's adultery, by reminding Othello that Desdemona 'has deceived her father, and may thee.' (ibid. p.26, l.290).

Brabantio speaks true; Desdemona deceived him by keeping her wooing of Othello secret. It is easy for a modern audience to overlook just how rebellious and indeed courageous an act this elopement of Desdemona's is. She is willing to defy her father and Venetian society in order to 'love the Moor to live with him,' (Shakespeare, W., (2005) p.25, l.246) and her character is defined with 'My heart's subdued/Even to the very quality of my lord,' (ibid. ll.248-9). Desdemona denies her father the conventional right for him to decide her future, and chooses to place her obedience in the hands of her husband.

Emilia too, displays duty and obedience to her husband, Iago, most evident in her taking of the handkerchief. She does this for Iago who has 'been so earnest/To have me filch it,', (Shakespeare, W., (2005) p.70, ll.312-3) judging the act to be above her duty to her mistress, despite knowing that Desdemona will 'run mad/When she lack it,' (ibid. ll.316-7). These duties are only reversed when the extent of Iago's villainy is revealed. He orders her to 'hold your peace,' (ibid. p.128, l.216) and 'get you home,' (ibid. l.221), which Emilia refuses to do though 'men, and devils,.../..., all cry shame against me,' (ibid. ll.219-220) for disobeying her husband so.

The idea of women as property is demonstrated in Othello's killing of Desdemona. Believing his honour to be impugned and his heart betrayed, Desdemona has made Othello 'A fixed figure for the time of scorn/To point his slow unmoving finger at,' (Shakespeare, W., (2005) p.99, ll.53-4). In Othello's tortured mind, Brabantio's warning has come true and 'she must die, else she'll betray more men,' (Shakespeare, W., (2005) p. 118, l.6). Othello justifies Desdemona's death not as 'A murder,' but 'a sacrifice,' (ibid. p. 121, l.65) he must make. His error realised and his fall from nobility of soul and position complete, Othello suggests a fitting epitaph for him would be to be called 'An honourable murderer,' (ibid. p.131. l.291) for it was to restore his honour that Othello killed Desdemona. It is telling that it is for the murder and attempted murder of Roderigo and Cassio respectively that Othello is to be arrested, not for Desdemona's. It is therefore, we must assume, Othello's right to execute an adulterous wife, but not her supposed lover, re-enforcing the double standard. For Desdemona's part, even though she declares her innocence, she does not dispute her husband's right to act against her, begging 'Banish me, my lord, but kill me not,' (ibid. 121, l.79).

A comedy differs from a tragedy in that it is not required to be a psychological study, but rather a plot that contains a series of coincidences, mistaken identities along with other stock dramatic devices and that stock characters can be used, for example Belvile is the conventional lover, Blunt the fool, Willmore the rake. Despite this, The Rover covers many of the same themes as Othello and holds the same values. Whilst women play a passive role in Othello, women drive the action in The Rover.

Like Desdemona, the sisters Florinda and Hellena in The Rover challenge male authority to determine their own futures. Florinda declares of her father's intention to marry her off as 'I understand better what's due to my beauty, birth and fortune and more to my soul than to obey those unjust commands' (Behn, A., (2010) p.265, ll.18-20). Hellena seems most unfit for a nunnery, for she loves 'mischief strangely' (ibid. ll.21-2) and is 'resolved to provide myself … a handsome proper fellow' (ibid. l31-2). Their father and brother ignore their natures and desires as being things of no consequence. It is here, in this opening scene, that the idea of women belonging to their male relatives as property is most notably demonstrated and shares this value with Othello.

To Pedro, though he acknowledges that

Belvile is a 'young and fine' (Behn, A., (2010) p.266, l.70) gentleman, that alone cannot make him a suitable husband for Florinda, for he argues 'what jewels will that cavalier present you with? Those of his eyes and heart?' (ibid. l.71) They are evidently fortune enough for Florinda who loves Belvile. The husband that their father has chosen is a rich man, and Pedro bids Florinda to 'consider Don Vincentio's fortune, and the jointure he'll make you.' (ibid. ll.66-7). Meanwhile, Pedro's candidate for Florinda's hand, Antonio, is 'brave and young, and all that can complete the happiness of a gallant maid,' (ibid. p.267, ll.131-2) and Florinda herself admits that she has no valid argument against marrying him, for 'I've no defence against Antonio's love,/For he has all the advantages of nature,/The moving arguments of youth and fortune.' (ibid. ll.143-5).

Though they have similar personalities and desires, the different values that men and women hold are most notably demonstrated by Hellena and Willmore. Willmore asserts that he pursues 'love and beauty' (Behn, A., (2010) p.322, ll.411-2) and this is his excuse, or reason, for his unbridled lust. In true rake character, every woman he comes across he tries to have sex with, sometimes forcibly, as in the case with Florinda. Hellena seems to share this lust for physical pleasure, but she counters his arguments for pre-marital sex with the realities of what that would entail for a woman, with 'what shall I get? A cradle full of noise and mischief, with a pack of repentance at my back?' (ibid. ll.417-8). Women are forced to consider the consequences of their actions in a way men in this period are not obliged to. Belvile calls Willmore 'a rover of fortune, yet a prince aboard his little wooden world' (ibid. p.324, ll.468-9), meaning his ship, which is conveniently anchored off shore, ready for a speedy exit. Pedro, who has his sister's honour and future to consider, counters this with 'What's this to the maintenance of a woman of her birth and quality?' (ibid. l.470). It is important to note that it is only the possession of a fortune that enables Hellena to finally decide her own future and snare Willmore as a husband. Pedro is glad to be rid of her for he is now 'free from fears of her honour...I have been a slave to't long enough' (ibid. l.484-6), her honour being the keeping of her virginity until she is married. Men here are responsible for maintaining honour in their female relatives, for, as in Othello, any slur would taint them and it seems to be a heavy responsibility.

Here we have two plays, written eighty years apart, one written by a man, the other by a woman, one a tragedy, the other a comedy. Yet they both show that ideas of the passivity and subordination of women were, in part, misconceptions and that honour, or at least the appearance of honour, were paramount. Shakespeare, of course, was unusual for his time in his understanding of womankind, but it is obvious from these two plays, that women and men did hold very different ideas about how they should be treated. What these two plays demonstrate is that men valued honour and the perception of honour, whilst women, while no less understanding of honour's worth and rewards, were prepared to make sacrifices and challenge society's rules to pursue independent desires.

Bibliography

Shakespeare, W., (2005) Othello, Penguin Books, London

Behn, A., The Rover in Owens, W.R. & Goodman, L., (ed.) (2010) Shakespeare, Aphra Behn and The Canon, The Open University, Milton Keynes, pp. 262-327

Owens, W.R. & Goodman, L., (2010) Shakespeare, Aphra Behn and The Canon, The Open University, Milton Keynes

N.B. *This was a Level 2 course. Note the in-text references. Here, quotations from the plays were simply given as l.470 - where l = line. This was acceptable at this level; however, a later Level 3 course that used plays, such as the Shakespeare: Text and Performance module, the way to quote from a play would have been 2.3.119, where 2 = Act, 3 = Scene, and the final number = the line number.*

8 EXAMINATIONS

Tutors, I think, have been programmed to persuade you that exams are wonderful opportunities to demonstrate your hard-earned knowledge of the module and that the stress they cause can be a positive force for good.

Poppycock - they're a form of mental torture that simply have to be got through.

If you read the forums when exam time is approaching, you'll see that many mature students start to panic about them. I did myself the first time I had an exam. I hadn't had to sit an exam since my A-Levels approximately twelve years earlier, and the not knowing what to expect, coupled with my own expectations and the expectations I imagined my family and friends had of me, led to my having anxiety attacks about this pesky exam which would take up just three hours of my life. I look back on it now, and I know I was silly for letting it get to me in this way, but that's the thing - stress isn't always rational.

For my first exam I got the average Grade 3 pass, and for the other two, Grade 2 passes, just what I was expecting – I knew I wouldn't be able to get Grade 1 passes, simply because all my coursework had been at Grade 2 level, but I was happy with Grade 2. When it came to my final module, I had a free choice - I could choose any suitable module at either Level 2 or Level 3 to complete my degree. I had already completed more Level 3 modules than I needed to satisfy the point system, so I decided to make things a little bit easier on myself by deliberately choosing a Level 2 course that was entirely coursework-based so I didn't have to take another exam.

Just something to note - you have to consistently produce exceptional work to get Grade 1 passes. Unless you're very gifted, I expect Grade 2 and 3 is what most people achieve, which is not at all bad when you consider that you're probably not just studying – you're holding down a job, looking after a family, and studying all at the same time.

Give yourself some credit.

Preparing for Examinations

When you start revising for your exam is really up to you. Some students start about two or three months before the exam, while they're still working on their final assignments. I personally found it difficult to concentrate on revision before I'd finished the final TMA, which left me with about a month to spare.

I must confess that my revision for exams was minimal. I was of the opinion that if I didn't know my stuff by that point, then there wasn't much hope for me. But I was studying for an English Literature degree, which did not require a perfect recall of exact names and dates, such as a History exam might, just an understanding of certain texts, their themes and devices etc. I expect other courses should be very well revised and I would not recommend my laidback attitude for them.

Basically, whatever time you have and however much motivation is left in you by the time the exam comes around, determines how hard you revise. As with everything to do with OU study, how hard you work is up to you.

■ You should work out how much time you have to revise

■ Whether you work better in short periods

of study, or in longer sessions

■ You should determine what you want to get out of the course

You may have been supplied with a Specimen Examination Paper (SEP) when you received your course materials, or you may be able to download one for your course from the OU website.

Have a look at this paper to familiarise yourself with the format of the questions so when you sit down in front of the real thing you will not be flummoxed. You can even practice the questions, timing yourself to see how you perform and how much writing you can manage within the 3-hour time frame. This is actually a very good idea, as so many of us use computers and type these days rather than writing, our hands have become out of practice. Writing trial essays in this way helps to train your hand to write for hours at a stretch.

Your revision strategy might be to just re-read your course books, or it might be to go through your essays, making short notes as you go. The notes you made during your coursework will probably be too detailed to be of much use at this stage, so go through and summarise them.

Your tutor will almost certainly provide you with helpful notes on revising, as well as letting you in on what subjects are unlikely to come up in the exam and so you need not revise. Other students, both former and current, are extremely good at posting their revision notes on the OU forums. Check these out as they can save you a lot of time creating your own. Just remember to thank the person for supplying them.

The Exam Itself

To prove that you are you and not someone else taking the exam for you, you must take the following with you to the exam:

- Your exam confirmation email or page from the website.

- A form of identification - a passport or driving licence is ideal.

Leave these visible on your desk as an official will walk around during the exam, checking details, and you don't want to be disturbed then.

When you get to the examination hall, there will be plenty of people there just like you - worried, nervous, and some attempting last minute revision. The hall will be set out like any examination hall, just like you remember from school, with individual desks in long rows. The exam papers will already be on the desks. The rows of desks will be divided alphabetically so you will need to find the row which represents the first letter of your surname. Your desk will have paperwork with your name upon it.

Check what you are allowed to use in your exam. In a Maths exams, you will probably be allowed a calculator. For other subjects, you may be allowed a dictionary, but definitely not the course textbooks or any written notes. You will not be allowed to have your bag at your desk so you should place this at the back or front of the hall, wherever you are pointed to. Just make sure your mobile is turned off inside your bag.

Always have a bottle of water on your desk, and it is a good idea to have a snack handy to stop your stomach rumbling or your mind turning to what you're going to have for lunch rather than focusing on your questions. A banana is a good choice, but if you have a bar of chocolate or cereal bar, unwrap it from its plastic wrapper before the exam starts so that you don't disturb other examinees during the exam.

If you need to go to the toilet during the exam, just raise your hand (again, just like being back at school) and tell an invigilator so. They won't accompany you to the loo, don't worry.

Once you are told the exam has started, you can open your question paper. Read through the whole exam paper and work out which questions you are going to answer, but don't linger over this. Time goes quickly in an exam.

If you are a planner, make a brief essay plan for each question, but get writing as soon as possible. Write as legibly as possible. Divide your time equally. Many OU exams are three hours long with three questions to answer. Obviously, in these cases each question should be worked on for an hour and no more, but you will need to work out your timing for exams that don't follow this format.

In exams where you have to write essays, I think it unlikely that you will have time or the energy at the end to read through your essays to check you have done what you need to, let alone rewrite sections that have veered off course. The good news is that after months of preparing and writing essays your writing skills are probably a lot better than you realise, and chances are you will produce a good, if not brilliant, essay. The examiners are aware that you will not be able to produce essays of the same quality as your TMAs, so don't worry too much about crossings out.

As we are very used to typing rather than writing, it is possible your writing hand will start to ache and cramp. You could practice writing for three hours at a time to train your hand. If you feel you need a break, even a short one, go to the toilet, whether you need to or not. Even five minutes can make the difference to your body and your brain. If you need more paper to write on, put your hand up and ask for more.

If you appear to be running out of time and it looks like you won't be able to finish your essay, then make some notes which indicate how you would have carried on had you had the time. This may earn you some marks, but these will not be at all comparable to those you would have achieved had you finished your essay, and it is, therefore, very important that you try to work within the specified time frame. If you make notes on your exam paper only to aid you in making your answers, such as a brief essay plan, make sure you cross them through to avoid them being marked.

You will not be able to leave in the last 15 minutes of the exam, so if you do get through it quickly and want to make an early exit, make sure it is before this time. At the end of the exam, you'll have to sit tight while the papers are collected, but then you'll be free to go.

Hurrah!

After the Exam

It's over. I know there are people who love to talk about the exam they've just sat as soon as they come out of the examination hall and online in the OU forums, dissecting each question, saying how they answered it etc.

Fine, if that's what you want to do, but I personally think there is little to be gained from comparing notes in this way. Frankly, after all the hard work you've put in, months of study, and a taxing three hour exam, don't you just want to forget about it, at least for a few hours? You're probably ravenous - go to lunch instead. Going over the exam with others will just throw up a load of issues you forgot or didn't cover. Nothing can be done about it, so why worry?

If, however, when you get your result, it turns out to be as bad as you feared and you fail, yes, of course, you will be upset. You may even feel stupid or worthless. But the truth probably is that you didn't revise enough, or the questions didn't cover the areas you felt more comfortable with. Or maybe, just maybe, you had a bad day. The Open University has re-sits, so if you do fail your exam, you'll have another opportunity to pass.

Prepare better, revise harder, cover a wider range of areas. You'll pass the next time.

9 AT THE END OF YOUR STUDIES

All qualifications from degree onwards will have a graduation ceremony, just like those at brick and mortar universities, with you wearing the cap and gown and your photo taken.

These are not compulsory, but it seems to me that if you've gone to all that trouble to spend years studying and improving yourself, you may as well shout about it, so I would recommend that you attend your graduation ceremony if at possible.

What You Are Now

You've completed all your modules, you've graduated with the qualification you were aiming for all those years ago. Well, what now?

If you did them to further your career, then you should do several things.

Firstly, if you have a business card, put those impressive letters you've been awarded (BSc, BA, MA etc.,) after your name.

Secondly, add your qualification to the top of the Education section of your CV.

If you have a blog, make a post announcing your graduation and the qualification you achieved. Share it on Twitter, Facebook, or whatever social media you use.

If you are on LinkedIn, add your qualification to your profile and announce it in any groups you are involved with.

But most importantly, for your own satisfaction and pride, frame your certificate and hang it on your study wall, along with your graduation photo. You worked hard for that qualification, so don't be shy about showing it off.

FROM THE AUTHOR

I have a favour to ask…

I hope this guide has been of some help to you in your studies with The Open University. If it has, I would be extremely grateful if you would post a review on Amazon and share it with your network on Facebook and Twitter.

Thank you.

Kate Scott

ALSO AVAILABLE

How to Write Essays:
A Guide for Mature Students Who Have Forgotten How

By
Kate Scott

Available in paperback and eBook from Amazon

Printed in Great Britain
by Amazon